This publication is intended for the educational interest c
intended to be the full or final authority on the subject ma... presented, nor is it
intended to substitute for supervision, consultation, or expert advice about mental
health assessment and treatment regarding specific cases or specific individuals.

Additional copies of these materials can be purchased by
contacting:

Indianapolis Grief and Loss Consulting & Educational Services

8306 Balmoral Lane
Avon, Indiana 46123
317-442-0289
Fax: 317-837-7754
indygriefloss@sbcglobal.net
Website: indygriefloss.com

ISBN: 978-1-934447-06-2

Dedication

This book is dedicated to all the participants who have had the courage to complete this program. We are deeply appreciative of your willingness to share your hearts and lives with us. We are thankful for the opportunity to share with others what you have taught us.

Paulette Walker, LSW
Michelle Shaffer, LCSW

Introduction

Dear Participant,

More than likely you have been given this workbook because you have experienced a painful loss of some sort in your life. Possibly you have even experienced multiple losses. Losses can come in many forms but most often are experienced through death, divorce, rape, abandonment, miscarriage, abortion and loss of childhood experiences. Losses wear many faces and come in many sizes, shapes and forms. The content of this material allows you to define your own personal losses. The feelings and emotions are very similar in all of these losses although the intensity of these emotions varies depending on the circumstances surrounding the loss and the relationship.

This material is not intended to take away the pain, but rather to walk with you and serve as a companion to you as you face the pain of grief. Our experiences for the past several years, working in the field of grief and loss, have led us to believe that each time you tell your story and share your tears, a little bit of healing takes place. It takes courage to share pain and grieve in a society that often values restraint.

We have also learned that it is vitally important to feel the pain as difficult as that might be. Healing takes place when we give ourselves permission to hurt and grieve. It is our hope that these lessons will encourage you to face the pain of your loss, identify your own personal strengths, set goals for your future and integrate your painful experience into your life story in a way that is meaningful and hopeful.

Paulette K. Walker, LSW
Michelle L. Shaffer, LCSW

Session I
This Is My Story

Be with those who are also grieving. As you
share your story, you will share an understanding
of the heart that is deeper than words.

Source unknown

Empathy

A desire to understand. Being aware of, being sensitive to,
and experiencing the feelings, thoughts, and experience of
another.

I can show empathy by _____

_____

"To show the ability to be sensitive and or responsive to another person's feelings,
thoughts or needs...to have empathy is not to tell someone their feelings are wrong
but to validate them...to have empathy is to relate compassionately to another
person's feelings...when a person has empathy they can share in another person's
feelings without becoming enmeshed"

Shelly Hellman, BS

Find Someone

1. Find someone who wears size 11 shoes._____

2. Find someone who knows what integrity means._____

3. Find someone who plays soccer._____

4. Find someone who is left-handed._____

5. Find someone who likes to draw._____

6. Find someone who plays an instrument._____

7. Find someone who hates pizza._____

8. Find someone who is the youngest in the family._____

9. Find someone who lifts weights._____

10. Find someone who sings in the shower._____

11. Find someone who can name five states._____

12. Find someone who likes to play basketball._____

13. Find someone who likes cherry pie._____

14. Find someone who can name the 1st President of the United States._____

4

Group Rules

Our group has adopted the following rules and guidelines:

1.

2.

3.

4.

5.

6.

7.

8.

I agree to honor & respect the rules and guidelines as set forth by our group members.

Signed:_____

Date:_____

Purpose of a Support Group

1.

2.

3.

4.

5.

Pain

The crisis and depth of pain are in the eye of the beholder.

Pain is stubborn

Pain is not pleasant

Pain will not be ignored

Pain does not go away with stuffing

Pain does not go away with denial

Pain does not go away with alcohol

Pain does not go away with drugs

Pain does not go away with pretending

Each person's pain is real, losses are different, no persons pain is more important than another's.

James Hendricks

It Hurts To Lose!

Loss-_____

Examples of loss:

1. Moving to another location
2. Abandonment
3.
4.
5.
6.
7.

Serenity Prayer

God grant me the serenity to accept the things
I cannot change, the courage to change
the things I can and the wisdom to know the difference.
Reinnold Niebuhr

7

A Broken Heart

The loss of someone or something important to us leaves us with a broken heart. It is important to allow our broken heart to bleed and hurt before we can begin the process of stitching up our wound. This is often a very frightening experience as we face the intense pain and allow our wound to remain open.

I have learned to cope with my losses in the following ways:

1.

2.

3.

4.

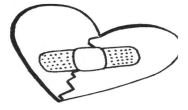

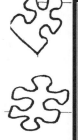

"Grief is like a jigsaw puzzle…I was all together
before the loss and now I'm trying to put my
life back together, but the puzzle
won't be the same because I am missing a piece."
Source unknown

Session I

"My" Story

Grief is a wound that needs attention in order to heal. Working through and completing the work of grief means to face feelings openly and honestly and to express and release those feelings. It also means to tolerate those feelings for however long it takes our wound to heal. The only grief that does not end is grief that has not been fully expressed. Take this opportunity to write your own story.

It takes courage to express pain! You have now taken the first steps towards the healing process.

My Thermometer

How Am I Feeling?

I have hurt for so long.
I have lost hope of
feeling better. I have
thoughts or a plan to
harm myself.

I am numb. I get
through each day, but
I am not sure how. I
hold out hope that I
will eventually feel
better.

I am experiencing mild
to moderate pain all day
with periods of
overwhelming sadness.
I can't eat or sleep well.

I am overwhelmed by
sadness for periods
of time each day.

I experience mild
sadness, sleep loss
and loss of appetite.
They seem to pass
quickly.

How I felt before
my loss.

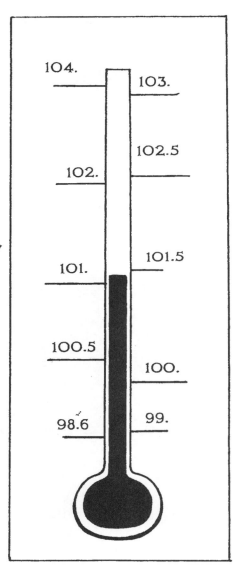

Suggested Response

Talk to a professional today.
Ask a loved one to stay with
you until you seek help.
List all of the people who need
you.

Talk to a professional. Ask
a loved one to call daily.
Take time to vent your
feelings and emotions in an
appropriate way. Write in
a journal.

Consider talking to a doctor
or professional. Ask a friend
to check on you daily. Set
aside 30 minutes a day to
be sad. Exercise daily.

Talk to someone you love
and share honestly how you
feel.

Give yourself credit for
acknowledging your pain.
Allow time to be sad as
needed.

My Gratitude Bank

Following each lesson, list something you are thankful for:

Session I _____

Session II _____

Session III _____

Session IV _____

Session V _____

Session VI _____

Session VII _____

Session VIII _____

Session IX _____

Session X _____

Session XI _____

Session XII _____

Session XIII _____

Session II
Grief Demands Our Attention

"Don't let anyone take your grief away from you. You deserve it, and you must have it. If you had a broken leg, no one would criticize you for using crutches until it was healed. If you had major surgery, no one would pressure you to run in a marathon the next week. Grief is a major wound. It does not heal overnight. You must take the time and use the crutches until you heal"
Doug Manning

Genuine

True, real, sincere, becoming transparent. Having no hidden agenda.

A person I consider to be genuine is:

_____

Can You Define?

Grief-

Grief represents the thoughts and feelings experienced within the person when they have a relationship with someone who dies. Grief is the internal meaning of our loss.

Examples:
1. Anger
2. Regret
3. Sadness

Mourning-

Mourning means taking the internal experience of grieving and expressing it outside of oneself. It is "grief gone public."

Examples:
1. Wearing black
2. Memorial wreath
3. Black wristband

Admitting Our Feelings

The feelings of grief are often very intense and frightening. It is important to admit our feelings. They are natural responses to a loss. Emotional effects can include:

Anguish ☐

Disbelief ☐

Denial ☐

Regret ☐

Sadness ☐

Loneliness ☐

Guilt ☐

Along The Road

I walked a mile with pleasure
She chattered all the way,
But left me none the wiser
For all she had to say.

I walked a mile with sorrow
And ne'er a word said she;
But oh, the things I learned from her
When sorrow walked with me.

Robert Browning Hamilton

Thought Processes

Before we recover from the pain of grief, we go through many different reactions in order to come to terms with our loss. Sometimes we have feelings or experiences that even seem unreal.

Some of these thought processes include:

1. Dreams of the deceased
2. Hallucinations
3. Sleep disturbances
4. Absent-minded behavior
5. Sense of presence
6. Preoccupation
7. Crying and calling out
8. Avoiding reminders of the deceased

Physical Sensations

1. Hollowness in the stomach
2. Tightness in the chest
3. Tightness in the throat
4. Oversensitivity to noise
5. Weakness in the muscles
6. Breathlessness
7. Lack of energy

Wounds do not heal without time and attention. Yet, too many of us feel that we don't have the right to take the time to heal from emotional and physical wounds.
"The Courage To Grieve"
Judy Tatelbaum

Does Anybody Care?

Often we find it difficult to communicate with a person who has experienced a loss. Therefore, we struggle with knowing words of encouragement and support to express in times of loss. Which of the following suggestions do you find appropriate?

_____I'm here and I want to listen.

_____It's probably for the best.

_____I feel for you during this difficult time.

_____This must be very hard for you.

_____Thing's could be worse.

_____You're young. You can get over it.

_____How are you doing with all of this?

_____I know how you feel.

_____You shouldn't feel so bad.

_____I care!

_____It was God's will.

**People don't care how much you know
until they know how much you care.**
John Maxwell

Grief Chart

Before we are able to recover from the pain of grief, we go through many different emotions and reactions in order to come to terms with our loss. These reactions can come in any order and any number of times.

- **Cross out** experiences you remember *already having had.*
- **Underline** experiences you're *currently having.*
- **Place a (?)** beside experiences you *haven't had.*

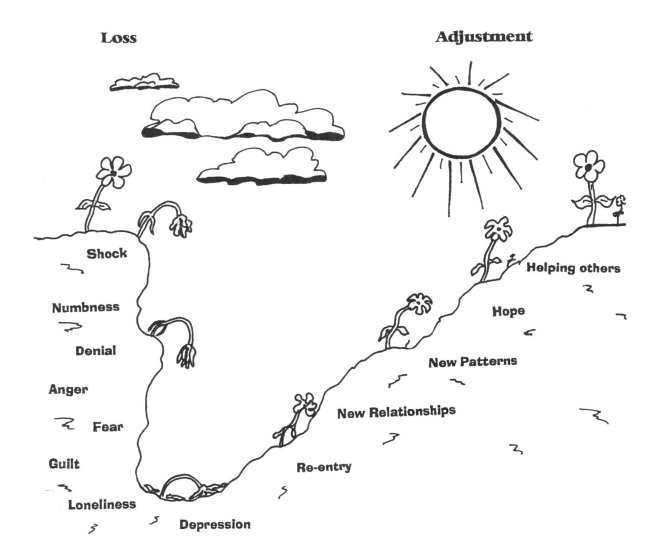

Loss

Adjustment

Shock

Numbness

Denial

Anger

Fear

Guilt

Loneliness

Depression

Re-entry

New Relationships

New Patterns

Hope

Helping others

Session III
Grief Is Complex

*You can expect to experience different stages in
your grieving: shock, numbness, denial, depression, confusion,
fear, anger, bitterness, guilt, regret, acceptance, hope.
They may come in any order and any number of times.*

Judy Tatelbaum

Courageous

Meeting danger without fear. Full of courage. The act of being brave.

I can be courageous in the following ways:

1.
2.
3.

Signs of Normal Grief

☐ **Sadness**
  - Most common feeling found in the bereaved.

☐ **Anger**
  - Frequently experienced after a loss. It can be one of the most confusing feelings and is at the root of many problems in the grieving process.

☐ **Guilt**
  - Guilt over not being helpful or kind.

☐ **Anxiety**
  - Survivor feels that they may not be able to take care of self.

☐ **Loneliness**

☐ **Fatigue**

> *No one ever told me that grief felt so much like fear. I am not afraid, but the sensation is like being afraid.*
> **C.S. Lewis**

My Feelings

	Yes	No
• I have felt feelings of sadness.	☐	☐
• I have felt feelings of confusion.	☐	☐
• I have felt feelings of disbelief.	☐	☐
• I have felt feelings of guilt.	☐	☐
• I have felt feelings of sleeplessness.	☐	☐
• I have felt feelings of anger.	☐	☐
• I have felt feelings of depression.	☐	☐
• I have felt feelings of loneliness.	☐	☐
• I have had difficulty concentrating.	☐	☐
• I often have a sense of emptiness.	☐	☐
• I often fear what the future will bring.	☐	☐

Broken Dreams
By Lauretta P. Burns

As children bring their broken toys with tears for us to mend I brought my
broken dreams to God because He is my friend.
But then, instead of leaving Him in peace to work alone I hung around and tried to
help with ways that were my own. At last I snatched them back and cried,
"How can you be so slow?"
"My Child", he said, "What could I do, you never did let go".

Dealing With My Feelings

1. The worst thing about my loss is_____

2. I get angry when_____

3. I feel lonely when_____

4. My feelings sometimes confuse me because_____

5. Guilt feelings come most often when_____

In your own words, describe the feelings you have experienced today.

Happy

Sad

Exhausted

Guilty

Enraged

Lonely

Hysterical

Confused

Angry

Depressed

Overwhelmed

Ashamed

HOW ARE YOU FEELING?

Session IV
Getting The Red Out

"When you find yourself doubting your
capacity to recover,
be patient and realize that the
grief process, though
lengthy, does ultimately
bring healing."
Judy Tatelbaum

Self-sacrifice

Giving up one thing for another. Giving up my own needs and
wants in the best interests of another.

Examples of self-sacrificing acts:

1.
2.
3.

I'm So Angry!

		TRUE	FALSE
1.	You may be surprised at the intensity of the anger you feel at times.	☐	☐
2.	The more senseless the act, the more anger we feel.	☐	☐
3.	You should not feel anger over your loss.	☐	☐
4.	It is possible to stop having particular feelings.	☐	☐
5.	Feelings of rage and anger are unacceptable.	☐	☐
6.	It is ok to be angry at family members, the person who died or abandoned you or God.	☐	☐
7.	It's wrong to feel vengeance.	☐	☐
8.	It's ok to feel angry at everyone who seems to be going on with life.	☐	☐
9.	What you do with your anger does not matter as long as you admit that it is there and don't hurt yourself or anyone else in expressing it.	☐	☐

10. Anger has great physical implications. If you try to stop yourself from feeling anger you may develop symptoms such as headaches, stomach aches or backaches.

☐ ☐

11. Even though anger doesn't feel good it is usually less painful than sadness.

☐ ☐

12. You owe it to your loved one to remain angry.

☐ ☐

Anger

Anger may recur again and again during the time we are grieving. Anger is a natural outgrowth of our sense of helplessness disappointment and our sense of abandonment by our loved one.
Judy Tatelbaum
"The Courage to Grieve"

The Many Faces of Anger

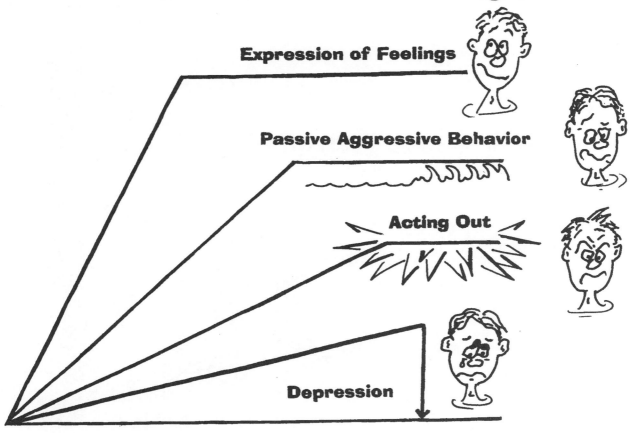

Acting Out
- Anger may explode, resulting in the use of sex, drugs, alcohol and destructive behaviors.

Expression
- The only acceptable way to diffuse anger.

Passive-Aggressive Behavior
- Smiling on the outside, yet angry on the inside.

Depression
- Turning anger inward. Anger is an epidemic in modern American society.

12 Common Triggers of Anger

- Insults, putdowns and name calling
- Not doing well at something
- Rejection
- Being teased or picked on
- Not getting credit for something
- Not feeling respected
- Unfair rules
- Hurt feelings
- Feeling powerless or not in control
- Frustration
- Not feeling loved
- Being unjustly accused

What Are Your Triggers?

MAKE YOUR OWN LIST

1. _____

2. _____

3. _____

4. _____

5. _____

6. _____

7. _____

8. _____

Warning Signs

- Tense muscles

- Loud or mean voice

- Fast heartbeat

- Fast breathing

- Feeling down or depressed

- Wanting to fight or break things

- Crying and withdrawing

To stay in control you must first know your triggers and warning signs. This makes it easier to use your anger to help you and not hurt yourself or others.

What Are Your Warning Signs?

1._____

2._____

3._____

4._____

5._____

The "SIT" Method of Keeping Cool

When your anger is "triggered" and your warning signs are flashing here is what to do:

- "STOP"   Tell yourself to stop so that you can gain your self control.

- "IDENTIFY"   Figure out why you are angry. Share your feelings with someone you trust.

- "TALK"   Once you are back in control, tell the person how you feel. Use "I feel" statements to express your feelings.

I feel_____

I feel_____

I feel_____

I feel_____

Reacting To Stress

Identify positive responses to coping with stress

1. _____ Discuss the problem and possible solutions with a friend.

2. _____ Eat well as part of your daily routine.

3. _____ Look and think like a loser.

4. _____ Take time to relax.

5. _____ Ignore the problem and pretend it will go away.

6. _____ Withdraw from people and spend a lot of time alone.

7. _____ Let your feelings rule over logical thinking.

8. _____ Give up and do nothing to solve the problem.

9. _____ Try alternative solutions.

10. _____ Be irritable and angry.

11. _____ Try alcohol or drugs to make the situation better.

12. _____ Deal with the problem without exaggeration.

Which 3 reactions best describe your usual response to stress?

1. _____ Positive_____ Negative_____

2. _____ Positive_____ Negative_____

3. _____ Positive_____ Negative_____

Dear _____

I feel angry because............

Session V
I Feel So Guilty

"Guilt is one of the most prominent and
uncomfortable feelings that interferes with the
successful completion of grief. So often we are
unwilling to forgive ourselves years beyond whatever
error we committed, or even when we are blameless."

Judy Tatelbaum

Self-discipline

Careful control and training of oneself. Careful regulation of
oneself for the sake of improvement.

When we are foolish we want to comquer the world,
When we are wise, we want to conquer
ourselves.

Source unknown

Guilt and Regret

		TRUE	FALSE
1.	Guilt and regret are rare experiences to a griever.	☐	☐
2.	We are so susceptible to guilt after a loss that we have the ability to turn any thought, feeling, experience, or memory into guilt.	☐	☐
3.	Being a "survivor" rarely provokes any feelings of guilt.	☐	☐
4.	During the grieving process "shoulds" and "if only's" rise to the surface.	☐	☐
5.	Frequently, we feel guilty about the last moments, days, or weeks of the relationship. We often regret something we did or something we failed to do.	☐	☐
6.	Unfinished business rarely appears in the form of guilt.	☐	☐
7.	Dealing with guilt is essential, for guilt can undermine self-confidence and delay one's recovery.	☐	☐

I Wish

Guilt and regret are common experiences of the griever, whether appropriate or inappropriate, rational or irrational. Feelings of guilt are often the key factors that keep people from adjusting and growing through the loss experience.

1. I wish I had said_____

2. I wish my loved one would have said_____

3. I wish I had not said_____

4. I wish my loved one would have not said_____

5. I wish I had_____

6. I wish my loved one would have _____

Grief is not an enemy--It is a friend. It is the natural
process of walking through hurt and growing
because of the walk. Let it happen. Stand up
tall to friends and to yourself and say,
"Don't take my grief away from me.
I deserve it, and I am going to have it."
Doug Manning
"Don't Take My Grief Away"

Dear_____

I feel guilty because.......

Session VI
Blueprinting Your Life

When a loved one dies we are confronted
with a profound challenge. We can either
give up or grow from the experience.
We can succumb to adversity or
use adversity to transform
our lives.
Judy Tatelbaum

Respect

Esteem, honor, showing consideration for, hold in honor.

A PERSON I RESPECT IS:

_____

Can You Imagine?

Can you imagine what it would be like to try to build a new home without a blueprint? Can you imagine what it would be like to go to the grocery store without a list of what you want? Can you imagine what it would be like to construct a home without a plan? This would not seem very smart. Where would you begin? Who would you call on the telephone to help you? Most of us would not consider building a home without a plan or blueprint. Why would we consider going through life without a plan or blueprint?

LARRY JAMES

Setting Your Goals

Your greatest power is choice. Your second greatest power is imagination. There are four important areas to consider when setting goals. Design your intentions in all four areas.

1. **SPIRITUAL GOALS.** Make this one your highest priority. Remember you can't do it by yourself. You need a support system.

_____

2. **FAMILY/RELATIONSHIP GOALS.** Never allow yourself to become so busy that you forsake your family or friends. Be with the ones you love. They need you now, not when you think you have time for them.

_____

3. **MENTAL/EDUCATIONAL GOALS.** You must consistently strive to be the best you can be. Read a good book. Put good "stuff" in your head. Work toward your education.

_____

4. **SOCIAL/RECREATIONAL GOALS.** Enjoy time with friends to recharge your batteries. You can often tell what makes a person tick by the way they unwind.

_____

Skills for Life

> "One's philosophy is not best expressed in words. It is expressed in the choices one makes. The process never ends, until we die. And the choices we make are ultimately our responsibility."
>
> Eleanor Roosevelt

- **ACCEPT RESPONSIBILITY** --- What do you think would happen if you made a commitment to be totally accountable to yourself for every aspect of your life?

- **BE COACHABLE** --- Being coachable is being teachable. To be coachable you have to want to be better. If you are not sincerely interested in being the best that you can be, you are falling short of your potential.

- **BE YOURSELF** --- Be honest with yourself. Stop pretending. Quit being a phony! People like to be around people who are real. Being yourself demonstrates self-confidence. When you love yourself, you can give love to other people.

- **PAY ATTENTION** --- Opportunities are everywhere. Look for them. Sometimes we are so busy being busy that we don't recognize opportunities. Learn to listen. Listening shows you care.

- **CONTRIBUTE** --- You are special! Every human being is unique. We are called to share our lives with others. Share your support, trust, love, enthusiasm, talents, ideas, faith, strength, loyalty and time to others.

Defining Your Purpose

- What is something that you could stay committed to for life?

- What is something that inspires passion within you?

- What is something that when everything seems to be going wrong you can hold onto during the difficult times?

- What is something that you know you can stand for?

- What is something that has you feeling you are making a difference?

- What is something that gives you the strength to continue?

A PURPOSE IS SOMETHING BIGGER THAN YOUR OWN PERSONAL WISHES. IT IS SOMETHING FOR WHICH YOU EXIST.
LARRY JAMES

MY PURPOSE FOR LIVING IS_____

_____

_____

> "Everyone has his own specific mission in life.
> Therein he can't be replaced, nor can his life be
> repeated. Thus, everyone's task is as
> unique as his specific opportunity to
> implement it."
> Viktor E. Frankl

My Personal Mission Statement

NAME_____

Describe your purpose for living.
_____
_____
_____

Describe your short-term goals.
_____
_____
_____

Describe your long-term goals.
_____
_____
_____

Describe what you choose your personal character to be. What strengths do you want to possess?
_____
_____
_____

Describe your responsibilities toward family, friends, self & community.
_____
_____
_____

Session VII
Guarding Your Conscience

"It is not what happens to us,
it is what happens within us
that will change the
world."
Mother Teresa

Character

Moral strength or weakness
A person I know of moral character is

_____

To be a person of moral character I must:

_____

I WOULD BE TRUE, FOR THERE ARE THOSE WHO TRUST ME;
I WOULD BE PURE, FOR THERE ARE THOSE WHO CARE;
I WOULD BE STRONG, FOR THERE ARE THOSE WHO SUFFER
I WOULD BE BRAVE, FOR THERE IS MUCH TO DARE.
I WOULD BE FRIEND OF ALL-THE-FOE, THE FRIENDLESS;
I WOULD BE GIVING, AND FORGET THE GIFT;
I WOULD BE HUMBLE, FOR I KNOW MY WEAKNESS;
I WOULD LOOK UP, AND LAUGH, AND LOVE, AND LIFT.
    By Howard Arnold Walter

How Does Our Conscience Work?

Define the purpose of *"Your Conscience."*

_____

_____

Psychologists who study the behavior of children tend to believe that the critical formation of our conscience takes place from birth through the 5th year. This process continues throughout life but the first 5 years seem to be the most crucial. Bonding and attachment take place when a child learns that he can trust others and others will care for him. Consequently, children learn to care for others and through this process the conscience begins to develop.

What happens if our conscience does not develop properly?

1. _____

2. _____

Goals of the Conscience

- As soon as you have two people the conscience is mandatory.

    Why_____

- The goal of the conscience is a healthy society.

    Why_____

- The goal of the conscience is an ethical life.

    List the benefits of living an ethical life
    1_____
    2_____
    3_____
    4_____

- The goal of the conscience is non-violation/integrity.

    Explain_____

People Without A Sufficient Conscience

True or False

1_____Lack sensitivity to others and violate the rights of others.

2_____Present a "nothing matters" attitude.

3_____Respect others at all times.

4_____Engage in random behaviors (just do it for kicks.)

5_____Give and receive affection.

6_____Invest in amusing images such as cruelty to others and pets.

7_____Find themselves preoccupied with blood, fire and gore.

"Experience declares that man
is the only animal which
devours his own kind......."

Thomas Jefferson

Building A Healthy Conscience

ATTACHMENT
- Children need a stable, non-needy person to attach to.
- Parents need to be accessible and display strong self-boundaries.
- Children need to attach to at least one other human being.

PRESENCE
- Children & teens need the presence of adults
- A conscience cannot be built through value free character building.
- The conscience must be built through adults who are value based.
- The self is grounded in things of value. Life is sacred.

MESSAGES
- Children & teens need clear consistent messages.
- Children & teens need consistent consequences.

STRUCTURE
- Children & teens need a world of "yes" and "no".
- Children & teens need the strong use of boundaries, rituals, traditions.
- Children & teens need progressive responsibility.
- Children & teens gain protection from boundaries.

CONSEQUENCES
- Children & teens need logical and natural consequences.
- Children & teens need consistent consequences.
- Children & teens need a progressive stress on choice.
- Children & teens learn from consequences.

EXPECTATIONS

- Parents need to maintain high expectations for children.

"MY" Conscience

To guard "my" conscience I must:

1. _____
2. _____
3. _____
4. _____

All of us need boundaries, structure and discipline for us to grow into emotionally healthy and responsible adults. We all have needs which can best be met by parents, family and/or those who are responsible for our care. List and describe your needs.

1. _____
2. _____
3. _____
4. _____
5. _____

"My Commitment"

From this day forth, I commit myself to work toward developing and guarding "my" conscience. I will strive towards refraining from all actions and behaviors that would be destructive or harmful to my conscience.

Signature_____ **Date**_____

Session VIII
Forgiveness is a Choice

Reconciliation isn't always possible, but forgiveness always is!

Resolve Through Sharing

Responsible

Accountable, reliable, the ability to distinguish between right and wrong.

A responsible person with whom I am acquainted is:
_____

To be a responsible person I must:
1. _____
2. _____
3. _____

Unresolved Conflict

Many illnesses can be triggered by unresolved emotional conflicts which take place in our life. Emotional stress can trigger all kinds of physical problems including ulcers, headaches and depression. The moment we begin to hate a person we become their slave. This person controls our thoughts and we have difficulty finding an escape from their grasp on our mind. The wrongs committed against us come in many sizes, shapes and forms. These hurts often come in two forms.

MINOR HURTS

Minor hurts are day to day bruises. They are not serious in nature. These kinds of hurts occasionally require a band-aid and a little time to heal. List some minor hurts you have experienced:

1. _____

2. _____

3. _____

MAJOR HURTS

Major hurts are far more serious. They cause great pain and require a lot more than just a band-aid to heal. They are often like open wounds and the pain is deep and lasting. List some major hurts you have experienced:

1. _____

2. _____

3. _____

Dealing With Our Hurts

WE CAN:

1. **Internalize** _____

2. **Retaliate** _____

3. **Forgive** _____

Write in the appropriate answer:

- We pretend all is well when it is not. _____
- It is an "eye for an eye" and "tooth for a tooth." _____
- It writes off the damage done to us. _____
- It hurls back stones which come our way. _____
- It is like a toxic waste, it poisons us from within. _____
- It causes resentment, bitterness and hostility in us. _____
- It seems so unnatural. _____
- It creates enormous pressure. _____

I deal with my hurts in the following ways:

- _____
- _____
- _____

Choosing Forgiveness

FILL IN THE FOLLOWING BLANKS USING THE WORDS FORGIVE OR FORGIVENESS.

We choose to _____ just as we choose not to _____. Extending _____ or withholding_____ is a clear and deliberate choice. _____ doesn't mean we feel better about what happened to us. _____does not mean the damage was not real or we will forget about what happened to us. _____ means we choose to release our offender from what is owed to us. Once we have made a choice to _____, the healing process is free to begin. Sometimes _____ brings instant relief. Often_____ takes time for our emotions to catch up with the action which our will has taken. We must grant a judicial pardon to our offender for the healing process to take place.

What actions can I take to assist me in making the choice to forgive?

1. _____

2. _____

True or False

1. _____Forgiveness always restores the relationship and repairs the damage.

2. _____Forgiveness writes off the damage that was done.

3. _____It serves no purpose to forgive someone who has not asked for forgiveness.

4. _____ Forgiveness is a feeling.

5. _____We choose to forgive by an act of our will.

6. _____ If we wait until we feel like forgiving, we never will.

7. _____ Extending forgiveness is easy and uncomplicated.

8. _____Forgiveness seems so unnatural and is an expensive thing to do.

9. _____The cost of forgiveness is always borne by the person who chooses to forgive.

10. _____Forgiveness takes place in our heart.

11. _____Forgiveness does not mean you endorse the other person's actions.

> *Forgiveness*
>
> *I ask today for help that I may forgive everyone in my life who has hurt me. I know that You will give me strength to forgive. I especially ask for the grace of forgiveness for that ONE PERSON who has hurt me most. I ask to forgive anyone whom I consider my greatest enemy, the one who is the hardest to forgive or the one whom I said I WOULD NEVER FORGIVE. Thank you that your will is to free me from the evil of unforgiveness.*
>
> *Author unknown*

"That's One Load I Choose Not To Carry"

The story is told of two men who traveled through life with sacks on their backs. Each time a hurt was received they would place it in what became known as their "injury sack." One man's sack became so bulging and heavy he couldn't walk without difficulty or pain. The other man's sack was empty and light. There was nothing in his sack. "How can your injury sack be empty?" a stranger asked. "Have you never been hurt?" "Oh, yes, I've been hurt many times," the man replied. "As my sack grew larger and its weight became unbearable, I asked my friend one day if he would help me carry the load." My friend replied to me. "No one can help you carry your load of hurt but there is a way for you to rid yourself of the pain. Take the scissors of forgiveness and slit the bottom of your injury sack. Your load of hurt will fall away." That is what I chose to do that day. Since then, I take all of the hurts which I receive and place them into my "injury sack" as before. But, now they simply slide out the bottom. Dr. Ralph Woerner

"That's One Load I Choose Not To Carry"

I place the following "hurts" into my injury sack. I choose to take the scissors of forgiveness and slit the bottom of my sack so my load of hurt will fall away. I choose to forgive:

1_____

2_____

3_____

Session IX
Change Begins Within Me

If we think we can guide our brother
aright, while our own feet still walk
in darkness, we are mistaken.
We must first clarify our own
vision, then we shall become
as lights, lighting the
way for others.

Ernest Holmes

Influence

Power of persons or things to act on others.

I can influence others by:

1. _____
2. _____
3. _____

> We do not deal much in facts when we are
> contemplating ourselves.
> Mark Twain

Dealing With Disappointments

Many times in life we are faced with circumstances and situations that are beyond our control. Sometimes we are responsible for our circumstances. Life is not fair and people often are not fair. Sometimes our role models in life have provided us with little direction. Sometimes we recognize changes need to take place within us. All of us need to re-evaluate our lives from time to time to reflect on areas in which we need to make improvements. Sometimes our lives have been filled with disappointments. These disappointments can guide and teach us very valuable lessons. What disappointments have you experienced in your life?

1. _____

2. _____

3. _____

4. _____

> **IF YOU ALWAYS DO, WHAT YOU
> ALWAYS DID, YOU WILL
> ALWAYS GET WHAT YOU ALWAYS GOT.
> IF YOU WANT SOMETHING DIFFERENT,
> DO SOMETHING DIFFERENT!**
> **Josh McDowell**

Disappointments Are Not Dead Ends

1. _____ are only delays. Who says that setbacks should be final.

2. _____ can be instructional. Lessons can be learned.

3. _____ are stop signs. They give us the opportunity to re-evaluate our lives.

4. _____ are merely obstacles. Clouds can hide the sunshine and disappointments can cloud our days.

5. _____ are necessary. They allow us the opportunity to develop faith, patience and perseverance.

6. _____ are tests. Everyone has roadblocks. The one who succeeds is the one who will not quit.

7. _____ can motivate us and give us the motivation to change.

8. _____ are normal. We all experience difficult times. We, by our reactions towards disappointments, can make them either positive or negative.

9. _____ are stepping stones. These stones can become a help or a hindrance depending on how we handle each situation.

Climb On Top Of Each Stone And Go Higher Toward Victory!

John Maxwell

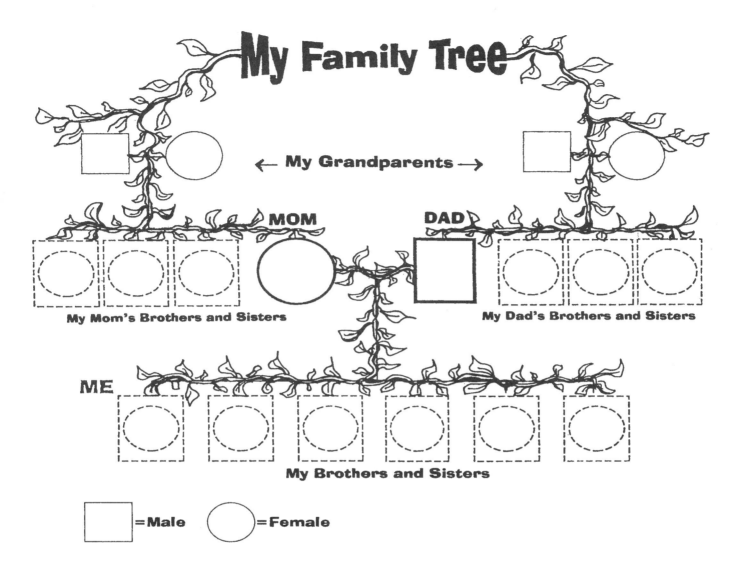

My Family Tree

← **My Grandparents** →

MOM   **DAD**

My Mom's Brothers and Sisters   My Dad's Brothers and Sisters

ME

My Brothers and Sisters

☐ =Male   ◯ =Female

INSTRUCTIONS

Draw in the males and females in your family tree. Outline each family member with issues listed below.

1. Drug abuse
2. Alcohol abuse
3. Teen pregnancy
4. Incarcerations
5. Physical/sexual abuse
6. High School Diploma

"I'VE LEARNED"

- _____I'VE LEARNED THAT YOU CAN DO SOMETHING IN AN INSTANT THAT WILL BRING HEARTACHE FOR LIFE.

- _____I'VE LEARNED THAT I AM RESPONSIBLE FOR WHAT I DO.

- _____I'VE LEARNED IT'S OK TO CRY.

- _____I'VE LEARNED THAT HEROES ARE THE PEOPLE WHO DO WHAT HAS TO BE DONE WHEN IT NEEDS TO BE DONE REGARDLESS OF THE CIRCUMSTANCES.

- _____I'VE LEARNED THAT SOMETIMES THE PEOPLE YOU EXPECT TO KICK YOU WHEN YOU ARE DOWN WILL BE THE ONES TO HELP YOU GET BACK UP.

- _____I'VE LEARNED THAT SOMETIMES WHEN I AM ANGRY I HAVE THE RIGHT TO BE ANGRY, BUT THAT DOESN'T GIVE ME THE RIGHT TO BE CRUEL.

- _____I'VE LEARNED THAT LIFE ISN'T ALWAYS FAIR.

- _____I'VE LEARNED THAT I CAN BECOME THE INSTRUMENT THROUGH WHICH CHANGE CAN TAKE PLACE IN MY FAMILY AND SCHOOL.

- _____I'VE LEARNED THAT YOUR FAMILY WON'T ALWAYS BE THERE FOR YOU BUT PEOPLE YOU AREN'T RELATED TO CAN TAKE CARE OF YOU AND LOVE AND TEACH YOU TO TRUST PEOPLE AGAIN.

- _____I'VE LEARNED THAT IT IS OK TO GRIEVE AND FEEL THE PAIN OF MY LOSSES.

- _____I'VE LEARNED THAT MY LIFE CAN BE DRASTICALLY CHANGED IN A MOMENT'S NOTICE BY PEOPLE WHO DON'T EVEN KNOW YOU.

- _____I'VE LEARNED THAT NO MATTER HOW GOOD A FRIEND IS, HE/SHE IS GOING TO HURT YOU EVERY ONCE IN A WHILE AND YOU MUST LEARN TO FORGIVE THEM.

- _____I'VE LEARNED_____

- _____I'VE LEARNED_____

It's Not Easy!

TO APOLOGIZE
TO BEGIN OVER
TO BE UNSELFISH
TO TAKE ADVICE
TO ADMIT ERROR
TO FACE A SNEER
TO BE CHARITABLE
TO KEEP TRYING
TO BE CONSIDERATE
TO AVOID MISTAKES
TO ENDURE SUCCESS
TO PROFIT BY MISTAKES
TO FORGIVE AND FORGET
TO THINK AND THEN ACT
TO KEEP OUT OF A RUT
TO MAKE THE BEST OF A LITTLE
TO SHOULDER A DESERVED BLAME
TO RECOGNIZE THE SILVER LINING
AUTHOR UNKNOWN

But It Always Pays!

Session X
The Gift of Friendship

"People don't care how much
you know until they know
how much you care."
John Maxwell

Integrity

**Firmness of character. State of completeness. When I have
integrity, my words and my deeds match up. I am who I am,
no matter where I am or who I am with.**

Who Do You Influence?

Sociologists tell us that even the most introverted individual influences thousands of people during his or her lifetime. We never know how much or who we influence. Our choice of friends often plays a vital role in the choices and decisions we make in life. Our friends often influence us to make good and bad decisions. Fill in the blanks to determine if the following sentences describe GOOD or BAD friends.

_____Friends really care about you.

_____Friends hurt your feelings intentionally.

_____Friends lie about you.

_____Friends listen to your feelings and will not make fun of you.

_____Friends encourage you to do constructive things which are good for you.

_____Friends tell you the truth and help you tell the truth.

_____Friends tell your secrets when they are mad at you.

_____Friends break a rule and let you take the blame.

_____Friends threaten not to be your friend if you don't do what they want.

_____Friends encourage you to be mean to others when you are mad.

_____Friends encourage you to face your problems no matter how scary the problems are.

_____Friends encourage you to drink alcohol and use drugs when you are lonely and sad.

List those with whom you have opportunities to influence:

- _____
- _____
- _____
- _____

How To Be Liked By Others

TRUE OR FALSE

1. _____ To have a friend you must be a friend.
2. _____ Always try to impress others rather than letting others impress you.
3. _____ The greatest hunger that people have is to be needed, wanted and loved.
4. _____ It's not important to always be kind to other people.
5. _____ Negative people attract others. Positive people repel others.
6. _____ Make fun of others rather than yourself.
7. _____ It is important to help people to like themselves. The greatest complement someone can give you is to say, I like myself better when I'm with you.
8. _____ Unless you can say something worthy about a person, say nothing.
9. _____ It is important to be a good listener. You can have a greater influence on others by the way you listen rather than by the way you talk.
10. _____ It is not important to like yourself.
11. _____ It is important to be genuinely interested in others. Get them to talk about themselves. Ask for their opinion, ideas and viewpoints.

List ways in which you can become a better friend:

- _____
- _____
- _____
- _____

Understanding Others

- Be tolerant of others. Learn to be patient and tolerant of other people's weaknesses, actions and differences.

- Avoid expecting people to be perfect. Have faith in people, believe in them, love them and like them. They come with a lot of good and a little bad.

- Be sure you WANT to understand people. There are times when you find yourself criticizing another person saying you do not understand why that person acts that way.

- Look for the good in others. It is amazing how we deliberately often seem to look for other's negative characteristics.

- Learn to love the unlovable. The personable popular individual with no irritating qualities presents no challenge to understanding. The challenge is to love the unlovable.

- Hate the thing and not the person. Understanding people does not mean you condone all of their wrongful acts and undesirable characteristics.

- Get all of the facts. Sometimes we do not know all of the facts in a situation when we are irritated with another person.

- Have empathy. You can never perfectly understand people, but you can imagine their feelings.

- Control your attitudes. Your reactions often cause negative feelings.

- Develop a mental image of understanding. Picture yourself as an understanding, patient, kind individual. Soon you will become that person.

Dear _____

Thank you for your friendship. I appreciate you because

Sincerely,

Session XI
Our Attitude is a Choice

So far today, Lord, I've done all right.
I haven't gossiped, haven't lost my temper,
haven't been greedy, grumpy, nasty,
selfish or over indulgent.
I'm very thankful for that.
But in a few minutes, Lord, I'm
going to get out of bed. And
from then on, I'm probably
going to need a lot more help.

AMEN
Source unknown

Attitude

An outward expression of an inward feeling or opinion.

Positive attitudes	Negative Attitudes
1. _____	1. _____
2. _____	2. _____
3. _____	3. _____

Choosing

Dr. Viktor E. Frankl, survivor of three grim years at Auschwitz and other Nazi prisons, has recorded his observations on life in Hitler's camps: "We who lived in concentration camps can remember the men who walked through the huts comforting others, giving away their last piece of bread. They have been few in number, but they offer sufficient proof that everything can be taken from a man but one thing; the last of the human freedoms---to choose one's attitude in any given set of circumstances, to choose one's own way."

True or False

1. _____ We cannot choose how many years we will live, but we can choose how much life those years will have for us.

2. _____ We cannot control the beauty of our face, but we can control the expression on our face.

3. _____ People catch our attitudes just like they catch our colds ----by getting close to us.

4. _____ It is improbable that a person with a bad attitude can continuously be a success.

5. _____ A leader's attitude is caught by his/her followers more quickly than his/her actions.

6. _____ We are not responsible for our attitudes.

7. _____ Life is full of surprises and the adjustment of our attitudes is a life long process.

8. _____ Many people who have suffered adverse situations in their lives become bitter and angry.

"Hardening of the Attitude"

"Your attitude and my attitude is a choice. We choose our attitude and we choose the way in which we think. We have a choice everyday regarding the attitude we will embrace. We cannot change our past and we can't change the fact that people will act in certain ways but we can change our attitudes. Our attitudes can become our most important assets in life."

JOHN MAXWELL

Take a moment and list the negative attitudes you possess that are possibly influencing others right now.

1. _____

2. _____

3. _____

4. _____

Take a moment and list the people who you have the most opportunities to influence.

1. _____

2. _____

3. _____

Attitude Adjustment

**"Your attitude and my attitude is a choice.
We choose our attitude and we choose the way in which we
think. Your attitude in life will determine everything you do
in life. It is not what happens to you, it is what happens in you
that makes a difference.
So, you are in charge of your attitudes."**
JOHN MAXWELL

Suggestions for Changing Our Attitude

- Identify problem feelings. This is the earliest stage of awareness. What are you feeling?

- Identify problem thinking. What are you thinking about?

- Identify problem behaviors. What triggers those wrong behaviors? Look beneath the surface.

- Identify right thinking. Write down thinking that is right and the thinking you desire.

- Make a public commitment to right thinking. Ask others to keep you accountable to right thinking.

- Develop a plan for right thinking. This plan should include:
  - A written definition of desired right thinking
  - A way to measure your progress
  - A person to whom you are accountable
  - A daily diet of helpful materials
  - Associating with right thinking people

JOHN MAXWELL

Attitudes

The longer I live,
The more I realize the impact of attitude of life.
Attitude, to me,
Is more important
Than the past,
Than education,
Than money,
Than circumstances,
Than failures,
Than success,
Than what other people
Think or say or do.
It will make or break a company...
...a church...a home.
The remarkable thing is we have a choice everyday
Regarding the attitude we will
Embrace for that day.
We cannot change our past...
We cannot change the fact that people
will act in a certain way...
We cannot change the inevitable.
The only thing we can do
Is play on the one string we have,
And that is our attitude.
I am convinced that life is 10% what happens to me
And 90% how I react to it.
And so it is with you.
You are in charge of your ATTITUDES.
By Charles Swindoll

Session XII
Becoming A Leader

Make me an instrument
of Thy peace.
Where there is hatred,
let us sow love;
where there is despair, hope;
where there is sadness, joy;
where there is darkness, light.
O Divine Master,
grant that we may not so much
seek to be consoled,
as to console;
not so much to be loved, as to love.
For it is in giving that we receive,
it is in pardoning that we are
pardoned,
it is in dying that we are born again
to eternal life.
Prayer of St. Francis of Assisi

Leader

Someone who leads the way. The ability to obtain followers.
Successful leaders

- **are willing to admit mistakes and accept the consequences, rather than trying to blame others.**
- **are able to get along with a variety of people.**
- **are sensitive to others and are calm and confident.**

Leader

Someone who leads the way.

- Leadership is influence.
- Leadership is the ability to obtain followers.
- Leadership can be taught.
- Everyone can become a leader

Examples of great leaders:

1 _____

2 _____

3 _____

My Influence

My life shall touch a dozen lives
Before this day is done,
Leave countless marks of good or ill,
E'er sets the evening sun.

This, the wish I always wish,
The prayer I always pray:
Lord, may my life help others lives
It touches by the way.
Source unknown

Am I True?

Billy Graham said, "Integrity is the glue that holds our way of life together. We must constantly strive to keep our integrity intact. When wealth is lost, nothing is lost; when health is lost, something is lost, when character is lost, all is lost."

To build your life on the foundation of integrity, use the following poem, "Am I True to Myself?", as a "Mirror Test" to evaluate how you're doing.

I have to live with myself, and so
I want to be fit for myself to know,
I want to be able, as days go by,
Always to look myself straight in the eye;
I don't want to stand, with the setting sun,
And hate myself for things I have done.
I don't want to keep on a closet shelf
A lot of secrets about myself,
And fool myself, as I come and go,
Into thinking that nobody else will know
The kind of man I really am;
I don't want to dress up myself in sham.
I want to go out with my head erect,
I want to deserve all men's respect;
But here in the struggle for fame and wealth
I want to be able to like myself.
I don't want to look at myself and know
That I'm bluster and bluff and empathy show,
I can never hide myself from me;
I see what others may never know,
I never can fool myself, and so,
Whatever happens, I want to be
Self-respecting and conscience free.

By Edgar Guest

A Most Important Ingredient

1. _____People with integrity have nothing to hide or nothing to fear.

2. _____A person of integrity does not have a system of values.

3. _____Integrity builds trust.

4. _____Integrity provides us a solid reputation.

5. _____Integrity does not demand us to live by high standards.

6. _____Integrity means living it myself before leading others.

CONSISTENCY: Are you the same person no matter who you are with?   Yes_____ No_____

CHOICES: Do you make decisions that are best for others when another choice would benefit you?
Yes_____ No_____

CREDIT: Are you quick to recognize others for their efforts and contributions to your life?
Yes_____ No_____

"The measure of a man's real character is what he would do if he would never be found out."
THOMAS MACAULEY

Successful People

A study of three hundred highly successful people, such as Franklin Delano Roosevelt, Helen Keller, Winston Churchill, Albert Einstein, Fanny Crosby and Abraham Lincoln reveals that one-fourth had handicaps, such as blindness, deafness, or crippled limbs. Three-fourths had either been born in poverty, came from broken homes, or at least came from exceedingly tense or disturbed situations.

Describe how you think these great achievers were able to overcome their problems.

_____

_____

_____

What situations and circumstances must you overcome to become a positive leader in your family and community?

_____

_____

_____

My Strengths

All of us possess strengths which enable us to become effective leaders. Sometimes we fail to recognize our strengths and utilize them in appropriate ways. Place a check by the strengths you feel you possess.

_____ **Patience**
_____ **Courage**
_____ **Empathy**
_____ **Self-sacrificial**
_____ **Disciplined**
_____ **Integrity**
_____ **Honesty**
_____ **Generous**
_____ **Hard-working**
_____ **Forgiving**
_____ **Understanding**
_____ **Accepting**
_____ **Loving**

Ask yourself the following questions as a means of self-evaluation to determine areas for improvement.

_____ Am I living like a loser?

_____ Am I lazy? Am I simply not requiring enough of myself?

_____ Is my life a dead-end journey, heading nowhere?

_____ Am I scared? Am I playing this game with sweaty palms?

_____ Do I have no goals? Am I just going through the motions?

_____ Am I continually making promises to myself that I never, ever keep?

The Little Chap Who Follows Me

A careful man I want to be,
A little fellow follows me;
I do not dare to go astray
For fear he'll go the self-same way.

I cannot once escape his eyes.
Whate'er he sees me do he tries.
Like ME he says he's going to be
That little chap who follows me.

I must remember as I go
Through summer suns and winter snows,
I am building for the years to be
That little chap who follows me.

Source unknown

I choose to be a leader because:

_____
_____

_____Yes, I choose to make a difference in
my family and my community.

Session XIII

"Letting Go" Ceremony

Dear Group Participant,

Congratulations on completing the "Growing Through Loss" program. It takes courage to feel and express the pain of grief in a society that often values restraint. The loss of someone important to us or something of value leaves us a changed person.

Today, your achievements are honored in the form of a "Letting Go" Ceremony. It is our hope that you will share your mission statements and poetry with others who choose to participate in your ceremony. It is also our hope that you will choose to make a commitment to be the one who will make a difference in your family and your community as a result of your loss experience. Our community is desperate for people such as yourself who have courage and choose to use their painful experiences to help those in need. Hopefully, by the completion of this program, you have identified personal strengths that will assist you in making a difference.

If you feel this program has been of help to you, we invite and encourage you to contact us and share your experiences. We always appreciate hearing your stories.

Best wishes,
Paulette Walker, LSW
Indianapolis Grief & Loss Consulting & Educational Services

"Letting GO"

To LET GO doesn't mean to stop caring. It means I can't do it for someone else.

To LET GO is not to cut myself off. It's the realization that I don't control another.

To LET GO is not to enable, but to allow learning from natural consequences.

To LET GO is to admit powerlessness, which means the outcome is not in my hands.

To LET GO is not to try to change or blame another. I can only change myself.

To LET GO is not to care for, but to care about.

To LET GO is not to fix, but to be supportive.

To LET GO is not to judge, but to allow another to be a human being.

To LET GO is not to be in the middle arranging all the outcomes, but to allow others to affect their own outcomes.

To LET GO is not to be protective; it is to permit another to face reality.

To LET GO is not to deny but to accept.

To LET GO is not to nag, scold, or argue, but to search out my own shortcomings and to correct them.

To LET GO is not to adjust everything to my desires but to take each day as it comes and to cherish the moment.

To LET GO is not to criticize and regulate anyone but to try to become what I dream I can be.

To LET GO is not to regret the past but to grow and live for the future.

To LET GO is to fear less and love more.

I Let Go

I reach down inside to the feet of my soul

And I take hold of the pain I have walked in so long.

And I bring it to my knees, which have helped hold this walk.

I stop at my hips, which have carried these emotions from side to side, from time to time. I bring them to my stomach where I have just taken and taken and taken; digesting the hurt and sorrows, making it run through the very depths of me. And feeds my spirit with grief and despair. Next, I stop at my heart where this pain comes alive with every thump and beat of my heart. I then go to my shoulders; I can't understand why they are so heavy-so heavy. So, I travel on to my mouth that speaks unpleasantries, my eyes that see all of the negatives, and my ears that hear condemnation. I carry this all to my mind and I then realize through learning and yielding and learning and yielding and learning and yielding.

I HAVE BEEN SET FREE!

So, I raise my arms and hands in VICTORY and I CLAP my hands. With all the hurt, the pain, the sorrow, the sadness, despair, shame and everything else that tainted me,

"I LET GO"

By Linda Johnson, Growing Through Loss Facilitator
Indiana Women's Prison
Indianapolis, Indiana

"Thriver" or "Survivor"

A "Survivor" blames the past
A "Thriver" plans the future
A "Survivor" finds fault
A "Thriver" finds solutions
A "Survivor" justifies "why not"
A "Thriver" discovers "why"
A "Survivor" points the finger
A "Thriver" is accountable
A "Survivor" stays out of trouble
A "Thriver" takes a stand

Now, more than ever, we need to come from a place of "thriver" and not just "survivor." A "thriver" would be the end result of recovering from significant loss, through grief and loss counseling. Is it enough to be a survivor or can we reach beyond that? Do we want to be planning our future or would we rather be blaming the past? Do we want to dwell on what has happened or choose to let those experiences propel us into new and positive ways of being? I choose to be a "thriver" and meet my challenges face on. I choose to be a mover and a shaker, and I challenge you to be the same. Come and go with me!

By Margo
"Growing Through Loss" Participant
Indianapolis, Indiana

Yes!

I will be the one to make a difference

_____
Name

_____
Witness

_____
Date

"People don't care how much you know
until they know how much you care."

John Maxwell